# Why Does God Allow Suffering?

## Ralph O. Muncaster

HARVEST HOUSE PUBLISHERS
Eugene, Oregon 97402

*Cover by Terry Dugan Design, Minneapolis, Minnesota*

**A Special Thanks** to Karen Bell-Wilcox for her endless hours spent contributing to the perspectives in this book and for her ministry contribution. Karen is a major leader in Strong Basis to Believe Ministries and has been involved in the research of several ministry topics. Karen is a CPA with a master's degree in business administration and has also pursued advanced studies in such diverse sciences as chemistry, biology, and physics.

## By Ralph O. Muncaster

Can Archaeology Prove the New Testament?
Can Archaeology Prove the Old Testament?
Can We Know for Certain We Are Going to Heaven?
Can You Trust the Bible?
Creation vs. Evolution
Creation vs. Evolution Video
Does the Bible Predict the Future?
How to Talk About Jesus with the Skeptics in Your Life
How Do We Know Jesus Is God?
Is the Bible Really a Message from God?
Science—Was the Bible Ahead of Its Time?
What Is the Proof for the Resurrection?
How Is Jesus Different from Other Religious Leaders?
What Really Happened Christmas Morning?
What Really Happens When You Die?
Why Does God Allow Suffering?

**WHY DOES GOD ALLOW SUFFERING?**
Examine the Evidence Series

Copyright © 2001 by Ralph O. Muncaster
Published by Harvest House Publishers
Eugene, Oregon 97402

Library of Congress Cataloging-in-Publication Data

Muncaster, Ralph O.
    Why does God allow suffering? / Ralph O. Muncaster.
        p. cm. — (Examine the evidence series)
    Includes bibliographical references.
    ISBN 0-7369-0608-8
        1. Theodicy. I. Suffering—Religious aspects—Christianity. I. Title

BT160 .M86 2001
231'.8—dc21                                                    00-046120

**Printed in the United States of America.**

02 03 04 05 06 07 08 09 10 / BP / 10 9 8 7 6 5 4 3

# Contents

God Allows Suffering—But Why? ............................................. 4

The Key Issues ................................................................. 7

Why Consider the Bible an Authority? ..................................... 8

God's Existence Is Evidenced by His Creation .......................... 12

God's Existence Is Evidenced by His Word .............................. 14

Why Did God Create Humans? ............................................. 16

Why Did God Create This Kind of Earth? ................................ 18

If God Is All-Powerful and Loving, How Do We
    Reconcile This with the Existence of Evil? ........................... 20

Why Did God Create a World He Knew
    Would Become Evil? ....................................................... 22

What Causes Suffering? ..................................................... 24

Are Suffering and Death Always Bad? .................................... 26

The Suffering of Jesus ...................................................... 28

The Suffering of Early Christians .......................................... 30

Placing Suffering in Perspective .......................................... 32

Suffering from Natural Disasters and Accidents ....................... 35

Why Does God Let Children Suffer? ...................................... 38

Suffering from Grief ......................................................... 40

Attitudes Affect Suffering .................................................. 42

Dealing with Suffering ...................................................... 44

The Critical Questions ...................................................... 46

Notes ........................................................................... 48

Bibliography .................................................................. 48

# God Allows Suffering—But Why?

### Is He unable to do anything about it?
### Or does He not exist?

As humans, we reason this way: "Why would a God who is caring and loving allow suffering to exist on the earth?" But in order to look carefully at all the evidence, we need to admit that our viewpoint is a *human* one and is *very limited.*

Many people refuse to believe that a God exists at all—let alone a God who really cares about human beings. Other people believe in a God—but their God stands above and apart from His creation and is indifferent toward individuals. Or they believe in a God who is part of everything in the universe, who is more a "force" than a person. Both of these kinds of Gods are impersonal, uncaring, and unloving. And at first glance, the existence of one of these types of Gods seems to fit with the chaos and suffering we see in our world.

But the questions then become, Why should an uncaring God create the universe, the earth, and mankind, if there is no caring or purpose behind His creation? Or where do we find any purpose *at all* in a universe where God is just an impersonal force contained in everything? These questions can be more difficult to face and understand than the problem of why a loving God allows suffering.

Then some people believe in the God of the Bible. This God is all-powerful. Even though He allows suffering (which actually serves a purpose), nonetheless He is:

1. Holy

2. Just

3. Loving and forgiving

If there is no God at all, we have no eternal hope, and we are entirely at the mercy of the world today, with all its evil.

(However, humans have always known instinctively that *some* God exists. There are very few *true* atheists.)

If an impersonal creator exists who is indifferent to His creation, or who is merely a "force" that is part of all things in the cosmos, then our response to Him (or It) has no significance, eternal or otherwise. After all, such a God wouldn't care about what we might say to Him.

But if a personal God exists, then nothing in life would be more important than coming to an understanding of a God like this. Why? Because a personal God such as the God of the Bible would love, care for, and have a plan for His creation. And in this case, we should know that plan and know how God wants us to fit into it. Such a plan would help us today—and probably for eternity.

We do not have to face the question as to whether human suffering exists. *It does.* But unfortunately, many people use the existence of human suffering as an excuse to justify their lack of belief in God—without ever examining the *role* of suffering. The real question is this: *Would any kind of God who is personal allow the suffering we see around us to exist? If so, why?*

Since we are mortal, bound by the three dimensions of space and by time, we could never totally understand a God who is beyond our dimensions, a God who could create everything that exists. However, the Bible gives us many insights into why a loving God would allow suffering. This book will look at those insights and consider the role that suffering has in our lives; it will also help us understand why this universe is the *best* universe that God could have created, in spite of all the suffering and difficulty we see around us.

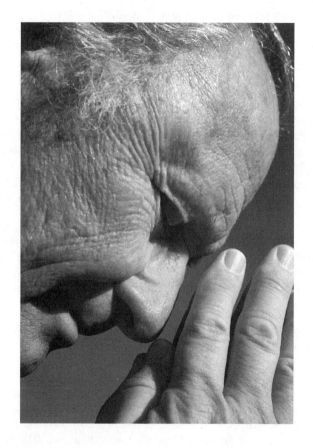

# The Key Issues

**1. Does an All-Powerful God Exist?**

This question has been asked since the beginning of the human race. All cultures show evidence of a belief in God that goes back to this beginning (though the traditions of some cultures also suggest the existence of an equal counterpart to God who is evil—a belief known as "dualism"). The Bible is the only written resource "proven" to contain information about God[1,2,3] (see pages 8–15), and it clearly indicates both the existence and the all-powerful nature (omnipotence) of God. He has no equal, and evil will not prevail in the end.

**2. Is God Personal?**

Some people believe that God is merely a "cosmic force" that neither cares about nor interacts with human beings, since He (or It) has no personality. Again, we need to start with a "provable" base of information—the Bible[1,2,3] (see pages 8–15 to find out how we can be certain the Bible is the only source inspired by God). The Bible is reliable, and it tells us that a very personal God exists (John 3:16).

**3. Is God Loving?**

Even the Bible portrays God as unloving, according to some people. For instance, they say, God allowed and even brought severe punishment upon humans. However, this idea needs to be reviewed within the context of the entire character of God—who is holy, just, *and* loving. Often these judgments were actually very loving acts, when we consider them from the perspective of humanity as a whole. The Bible clearly declares that God is Love (1 John 4:7,8—also see pages 24–33).

**4. Then Why Would God Allow Pain and Suffering to Exist?**

Most people would agree that some pain is good. For example, it can warn us that we are sick and teach us to avoid touching hot stoves. It is the much more difficult-to-understand, seemingly "senseless" suffering allowed by God that is the focus of the questions in this book.

# Why Consider the Bible an Authority?

There is vast evidence, including statistical proof, that an all-knowing God inspired the Bible.* Here is a short summary with some examples.

## 1. The Bible's Prophecies[2]

*One-hundred-percent accurate* historical prophecy provides irrefutable "proof" that a God from beyond time and space inspired the Bible. Why? Because there are well over 600 historical (thus verifiable) prophecies contained in the Bible—with none ever shown to be wrong. The odds of this happening without the involvement of God are inconceivable—considered "absurd" by statisticians. For example, just 48 of the prophecies about Jesus coming true in any one person by coincidence is like winning 22 state lotteries in a row with the purchase of one ticket for each. Put another way, the odds are similar to those of one person being struck by lightning 31 times.[2] Since these prophecies were written hundreds of years before Jesus' birth (which has been confirmed by archaeology), we know they were not contrived after the events. The prophecies were extremely specific, giving names of people, places, timing, and specific descriptions of unusual events. No other purported holy book contains even a few miraculous prophecies, let alone the hundreds found in the Bible.

## 2. Scientific Insights[3]

Similar irrefutable evidence of the divine inspiration of the Bible is found in more than 30 amazing scientific insights recorded in the Bible more than 2000 years before science discovered them. The biblical writings are accurate in their references to:

- Physics—the first and second laws of thermodynamics, and more
- Engineering—the ideal dimensions of the ark for its purpose

---

* This evidence is presented in the *Examine the Evidence* books listed in the Notes and Bibliography.

- Geology—the hydro-logic cycle, ocean currents, atmospheric phenomena, and more
- Astronomy—the earth is suspended in space, the earth is round, the difference between stars, and more
- Medicine—quarantine, sanitation, handling of the dead, and more

The Bible was not intended to be a science text, but a guide to human relationships with God. Even so, its references to science are all correct—though recorded centuries in advance of our time.

## The Accuracy of the Creation Account

Scientists who thoroughly analyze the ten steps of creation described in Genesis 1 find that the order of the steps listed agrees with the order discovered by science.[3]

Point 1—When Moses recorded the events of creation in about 1500 B.C., no culture had any scientific knowledge about the universe, the conditions of the earth, or the animals, or how any of them were formed.

Point 2—At the time of Moses, no culture knew the *order* of the events of creation. The odds of just guessing the order correctly (even if the steps were known) is about one chance in four million—similar to the odds of winning a state lottery.

Was Moses just extremely lucky at guessing both the steps and the order? Or was he inspired by God?

## 3. Reliability of Biblical Manuscripts[4]

The original Old Testament manuscripts were holy Scripture—that is, a written record of words inspired by God. So vital was the accuracy of Scripture that any person claiming to speak for God who said anything that didn't prove to be true was to be put to death (Deuteronomy 18:20). Scribes—those whose profession was to copy the Bible—were highly respected and had many years of rigorous training. Many time-consuming cross-checks were made to ensure the accuracy of their work.[5]

Furthermore, the people of Israel memorized vast sections of Scripture, even entire scrolls. So any mistakes that might appear were quickly corrected. The miraculous accuracy of the Old Testament

Scriptures was confirmed in 1947, when scrolls of all the books of the Old Testament (except Esther) were found—untouched for nearly 2000 years. Some of these "Dead Sea Scrolls" date back to nearly 300 B.C. All are virtually identical to the most recent Old Testament Hebrew texts.

Likewise, the reliability of the New Testament is shown by the more than 24,000 manuscripts from the early centuries of the church that are still in existence today. Though many of these manuscripts were not copied by highly trained scribes, there is still little difference among the thousands of copies. Moreover, the age of the manuscripts demonstrates that the New Testament writings were in wide circulation during the time of the eyewitnesses to the events recorded. These eyewitnesses would not have tolerated widespread proliferation of errors.

# 4. Historical Accuracy[5, 6, 7]

The historical accounts in the biblical record display both precision and accuracy. In the late 1800s, it was widely believed that the Bible was full of historical errors. But when the world's most renowned archaeologists began to investigate the Bible, expecting to prove it wrong, they instead found it accurate to the smallest detail. Now the Bible is regarded as a major historical source for archaeology in the Middle East. Using the Bible, archaeologists of many different religions have discovered entire cities and cultures whose existence had been long forgotten.

Especially important are archaeological finds that support the God-inspired prophecies of the Bible. The Dead Sea Scrolls (see above) are but one example. Early copies of the Septuagint (a translation of Scripture made from Hebrew to Greek in about 280 B.C.) and other early translations also confirm prophetic texts. One of the most amazing prophecy-confirming finds was the "Cyrus cylinder," which records King Cyrus of Persia's decree allowing the return of the Israelites from exile. This decree had been prophesied by Isaiah about 200 years earlier—long before Cyrus was born (Isaiah 44:28). Archaeological evidence that confirms other prophecies from both the Old and New Testaments is abundant.

## Non-Christian Evidence of Jesus' Existence

Critics sometimes maintain that all written evidence of Jesus Christ comes from biblical Christian writings, which they dismiss as biased. However, these writings must be reckoned with for many historical reasons, especially the willingness of many of the eyewitnesses of the events to die martyrs' deaths to defend the written record. The martyrdom of these early Christians is supported by many archaeological finds.

Furthermore, there are many non-Christian writings that refer to Jesus, His miracles, His crucifixion, and belief in His resurrection. The sources include:

- Josephus
- Cornelius Tacitus
- Hadrian
- Phlegon
- Mara Bar-Serapion
- Thallus
- Pliny the Younger
- Suetonius
- Lucian of Samosata
- The Jewish Talmud

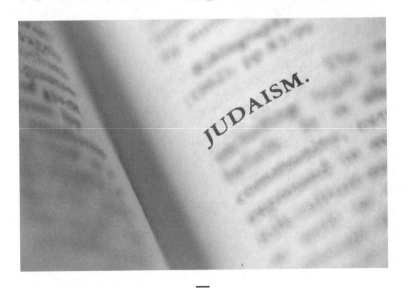

# God's Existence Is Evidenced by His Creation

The Bible says that God's existence, as evidenced by His earthly creation, has been obvious to humans since the beginning of time.

> Since the creation of the world God's invisible qualities—
> his eternal power and divine nature—have been clearly seen,
> being understood from what has been made,
> so that men are without excuse.
> —*Romans 1:20*

Whether or not we believe in the Bible, we should all ponder this verse. As an example of evidence in creation for God's existence, consider insects. As we view the amazing details of insects' bodies in photographs and on television, we are awed by the complexity of these seemingly simple creatures. Some have sonar, others radar; many have complex organs of hearing, sight, or other senses. And we are fascinated by the multitude of intricate body parts for chewing, attacking, defending, and reproducing.

When we learn about these things as children, God's existence is "easy" to understand; it seems natural to us. Jesus taught us to adopt that childlike attitude of innocent humility and trust in an all-powerful God (Matthew 18:3). Some great intellects have said that the people most likely to accept

## The Bible Says to See God in Nature

*The Bible repeatedly tells us to see and marvel at God through the world around us:*

| | |
|---|---|
| Job 10:8-14 | Psalm 98:2,3 |
| Job 12:7-10 | Psalm 104 |
| Job 34:14,15 | Psalm 139 |
| Job 35:5-7 | Proverbs |
| Job 37:5-7 | 8:22,33 |
| Job 38–41 | Ecclesiastes 3:11 |
| Colossians 1:23 | Habakkuk 3:3 |
| Psalm 19:1-6 | Acts 14:17 |
| Psalm 50:6 | Acts 17:23 |
| Psalm 85:11 | Romans 1:18-25 |
| Psalm 97:6 | Romans 2:14,15 |

and understand God are either little children or the greatest geniuses. As for the rest of us, our limited knowledge can actually hinder our understanding and acceptance of God.

And when we look at the heavens above, *it's hard to imagine no God*. The Bible says:

> The heavens declare the glory of God.
> —*Psalm 19:1*

## The Anthropic Principle

The anthropic principle is the term given to the body of findings that the planet earth, along with its surrounding galactic environment, is *extremely fine-tuned* for the existence of human beings and other life forms. Every year, several amazing new findings are reported. Following is a sample from a list of more than 100 characteristics of the earth. These represent only a very small portion of the great number of delicate balances necessary for life on our planet.

Life on earth could not exist if *any one* of the following were the case:[1,3]

- slower rotation of the earth
- faster rotation of the earth
- the earth 2–5% farther from the sun
- the earth 2–5% closer to the sun
- 1% change in sunlight reaching the earth
- a smaller earth
- a larger earth
- a smaller moon
- a larger moon
- more than one moon
- the earth's crust thinner
- the earth's crust thicker
- oxygen/nitrogen ratio greater
- oxygen/nitrogen ratio less
- more or less ozone in the atmosphere

# God's Existence Is Evidenced by His Word

## Prophecy Miracles and Scientific Insights

It has already been established that the vast number of 100-percent accurate prophecies in the Bible, in addition to the many scientific insights contained in it hundreds of years before science "discovered" them, provides statistical evidence that God inspired the Bible (see pages 8, 9). Applied mathematics experts and statistical analysts—and people who just simply acknowledge the utter improbability of winning the lottery hundreds of times in a row with a single ticket each time—all recognize that some supernatural power must have provided input into the Bible's descriptions and prophecies of future events.

## The Miraculous Composition of the Bible

How likely is it that we could assemble 40 authors, all from the same city, all with the same occupation, all from the same period of time, and have them write 66 books that all take the same viewpoint on the central issues of very controversial topics? Naturally, it seems extremely improbable, if not totally impossible.

Now consider the Bible. Here we have 40 authors writing 66 books over a period of many centuries—authors from different cultures, having various occupations, and writing under vastly different circumstances—and yet the Bible is still 100-percent consistent on a huge variety of controversial issues.* The only reasonable explanation is that the God of the universe intended these books to be written so precisely and consistently—by mere humans—that His existence and His interaction with us would be clearly demonstrated.

* See *Is the Bible Really a Message from God?* in the *Examine the Evidence* series.

# Miraculous Survival of the Bible

Never in the history of the world has any single holy book been so persecuted or suffered so many outright attempts to destroy it. Yet the Bible is by far the most well-documented ancient writing of any—and this includes all the ancient sources we use regularly as historical evidence. And the Bible has been the bestselling printed book every year since the early years of the printing press.

The codex form of the Bible (the book form, as opposed to scrolls) became popular soon after the resurrection of Jesus. The letters of Paul, the Gospel accounts, and the other New Testament books became the "enemy," first to the leaders of the Jewish religious tradition, and later to Rome. As a result, the burning and destruction of Bibles increased to a "flash point" in A.D. 64, the year in which Nero blamed the fire of Rome on Christians. This increased the pressure to destroy Bibles. And in A.D. 303, the Roman emperor issued an edict that anyone found with a Bible would be executed. Naturally there was a mass destruction of Bibles—but also a mass concealment of them. Then a few decades later the emperor Constantine made Christianity the official religion of the Roman empire. Destruction ceased. This put an end to about 300 years of massive attempts to annihilate the Bible, though even today some countries ban and attempt to suppress the Bible.

## Summary of Major Points

1. God exists—as evidenced by His creation.

2. God exists—as evidenced by the miraculous information contained in the Bible.

3. God relates to humans—as evidenced by His miraculous inspiration of the Bible.

# Why Did God Create Humans?

The straightforward answer to this question is that no one can be certain why God created humans, or for that matter, why He created anything in the universe. However, we can get some clues and indications from the Bible, which we have already established as an authority that gives us insight into the will of God (see pages 8–15). Here are some conclusions that we can draw from Scripture:

1. **Humans are uniquely planned by God.** How do we know this? First, God intended from the beginning that human beings would exist with Him in an eternal paradise forever (Revelation 21:3). Second, God created from a cosmic chaos an environment that is precisely right for the existence of mankind (the anthropic principle*—see page 13). Finally, we can see that, out of all the creatures God made to populate the earth, only humans worship Him—and they will continue to worship Him forever in heaven (Revelation 4:9-11).

2. **God created mankind in His image** (Genesis 1:26). In English, the word "image" often refers to a physical likeness. But the meaning of the original biblical Hebrew word is actually quite broad;[8] it can also mean a spiritual or other type of likeness. Therefore, God may have created humans with a "likeness" to Him in His qualities of love, forgiveness, justice, and many other areas, including the attribute of free will.

3. **God provided a means of redemption because He realized that humans would sometimes use free will for evil.** God in His perfect love allowed humans freedom of choice—a free will—which would allow corruption of His perfect creation by imperfect choices. However, God also provided human beings with a choice of redemption that would permit them to be reconciled with Him in all His perfection, even though they had misused their free will to make corrupt choices. The steps for humans to be reconciled with God are: 1) belief that God exists and that He came to earth in the form of Jesus; 2) desire to turn from evil (a confession of wrongdoing and repentance); 3) acceptance of the sacrifice of Jesus as forgiveness for their evil thoughts and deeds—that is, making Jesus their Savior; and

---

* See also *Science—Was the Bible Ahead of Its Time?* in the *Examine the Evidence* series.

4) sincerely asking Jesus (God) to take control of their lives, putting all of their trust in Him, thus making Him their Lord (see page 46).

4. **God wants perfect humans in heaven with Him forever.** Of course nobody is perfect, since all human beings have used their free will to make imperfect decisions. But the Bible tells us that any person can be "made perfect" through the sacrifice of Jesus (Hebrews 10:12-18). Though this is hard to understand, we have already established the Bible as a credible authority, inspired by God. Therefore we can trust anything that it says. So by choosing God's plan to reconcile Himself to an imperfect world (see pages 22, 23), any person can be made perfect and be afforded the opportunity to exist with God forever in heaven.

5. **Bottom line: God wants eternal fellowship with humans.** But because He loves all humans perfectly and wants only the best for them, He wants His fellowship with them to be based only on His character of perfect love, perfect holiness, and perfect justice. His perfect love brings Him to let humans make free will choices. His perfect holiness requires humans, if they wish to be forgiven of their evil, to choose to accept the sacrifice of Jesus. And His perfect justice requires humans to accept the awful consequences—hell—if they choose to not accept God's love.

# Why Did God Create This Kind of Earth?*

God's ultimate purposes for human beings are often mentioned in the Bible, our only reliable authority (see pages 8–11). Among His many purposes, God created the earth and its creatures for the dominion of human beings (Genesis 1:26-28). But His ultimate objectives for humans are that they:

- Freely love Him with all their heart, soul, mind, and strength (Mark 12:30)
- Worship Him forever (Revelation 4; 21; 22)
- Enjoy direct fellowship with Him (Revelation 21:3)
- Enjoy an eternal life that is beyond earthly imagination (Matthew 13:44-46)

## How God's Objectives Fit with the Kind of World We Live In

1. **God had to create something.** Otherwise His objectives could not have been expressed.

2. **God could have created a world without evil.** Humans could have been programmed to always choose the right and holy path. This would have resulted in a world of God-directed "robots." Love would not exist. (For example, if you programmed your computer to say "I love you" every day, would this be love?)

3. **Since God loves perfectly, and since He desires human beings to love Him perfectly in turn, mankind was allowed free will.** This gave human beings the opportunity to choose to love both God and others. However, it also allowed them the choice not to love. God's decision to allow free will resulted in a perfect world—but one that has been and is being used for imperfect choices.

4. **Though God created everything perfect, perfect things can be and are used for evil.**

   - Fire can heat or cook, but it can also injure and kill.
   - Nuclear energy can generate electricity, but it can also be used for bombs.

* See also chart on pages 22, 23.

- Metal can be used for many wonderful things, but it can also be used for bullets.
- Our minds can be used to help people, but they can also be used to hate people.

5. **Evil is a choice to misuse perfect things, thus bringing corrupt results**. Evil is not a "thing"; it is the *absence* of a thing—the absence of purity and holiness. It is the *mis*use of things that were created perfect and were meant to be used perfectly. In other words, evil could not be defined, nor could it even exist, if there were no holy, pure things in the first place. To give a couple of rough examples, if no sight existed, how would we know the evil of someone's gouging out another's eyes with his perfect thumbs? If humans had no legs to begin with, how would we know the evil of becoming paralyzed in an accident caused by a drunk driver—the result of misusing God's perfect gift of a body and a properly functioning car?

6. **A loving God could let everyone—even very evil people—into heaven**. After all, wouldn't that be perfect forgiveness and love? However, it would *contradict the other attributes of God's character*—His perfect holiness and justice—because evil would enter the holy place where God lives, and because it would be unjust—evil would not receive its proper penalty. Consequently, the world that God created required: 1) *choice* so that we can show perfect love for Him, along with 2) *redemption* so that His perfect justice and holiness can be expressed (Romans 3:21-26).

Through Jesus we can be "made perfect" (Hebrews 10:1-14). But we need to choose to turn from evil (repent) and accept Jesus as both Lord and Savior so we can gain His ultimate perfection. Jesus came to earth as a human, suffering all the temptations and trials of a human being so we could relate to Him. Then He allowed Himself to be executed in one of the most horrible, painful, and humiliating ways ever conceived by humans—to demonstrate God's great love for us and to provide forgiveness *for all who want it*. Rejecting, or not accepting, this free gift of love and forgiveness is the ultimate demonstration of lack of love for God.

# If God Is All-Powerful and Loving . . .

## Questions

**1. Doesn't logic imply that God created evil?**

- God created everything.

- Evil is something.

- Therefore, God created evil.

**2. Didn't God create imperfect beings?**

- Every being God made should be perfect.

- But perfect beings would not do imperfect things.

- Therefore, God created imperfect beings.

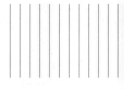

**3. Why can't God stop evil?**

- If God is all-good, He *would* destroy evil.

- If God is all-powerful, He *could* destroy evil.

- But evil has not been destroyed.

- Therefore, either God is not all-good, or else He is not all-powerful.

**4. Why does God wait to stop evil?**

- If God can and will stop evil, He would stop it.

- If God were all good, He wouldn't wait to stop evil.

- Yet evil continues to exist.

- Therefore, either God is not all-good, or else He cannot stop evil.

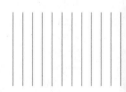

# . . . How Do We Reconcile This with the Existence of Evil?[5]

## Answers

1. No. Evil is a *lack* of the pure and holy use of things—not a "thing."

   • God created *everything* pure and holy.

   • Evil is not a thing—it is the *misuse* of pure and holy things.

   • Therefore, God did not create evil. Humans chose to misuse pure and holy things—thus causing evil.

2. **Perfect love requires freedom of choice, thus allowing the possibility of evil.**

   • God originally made everything perfect, including love.

   • Perfect love requires a free-will choice—including freedom to not love and freedom to do evil.

   • Therefore, God did not create imperfect beings. His creation uses free will to choose to do evil.

3. **Evil can and will be stopped.**

   • Since God is all-good, He *will* destroy evil.

   • Since God is all-powerful, He *can* destroy evil.

   • But evil is not yet destroyed.

   • Therefore, one day God will destroy evil.

4. **God waits to destroy evil to allow more people to be saved.**

   • God could stop evil now, yet He allows it to continue.

   • When God destroys evil, free will also will be stopped.

   • When free will is stopped, the *choice* to love God stops.

   • Therefore, God will stop evil when His will for people to be saved is completed.

# Why Did God Create a World . . .

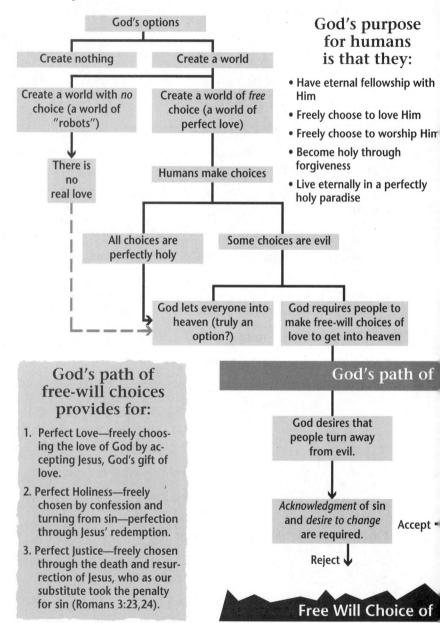

**God's options**

Create nothing | Create a world

Create a world with *no* choice (a world of "robots") | Create a world of *free* choice (a world of perfect love)

There is no real love

Humans make choices

All choices are perfectly holy | Some choices are evil

God lets everyone into heaven (truly an option?) | God requires people to make free-will choices of love to get into heaven

**God's purpose for humans is that they:**

- Have eternal fellowship with Him
- Freely choose to love Him
- Freely choose to worship Him
- Become holy through forgiveness
- Live eternally in a perfectly holy paradise

**God's path of free-will choices provides for:**

1. Perfect Love—freely choosing the love of God by accepting Jesus, God's gift of love.
2. Perfect Holiness—freely chosen by confession and turning from sin—perfection through Jesus' redemption.
3. Perfect Justice—freely chosen through the death and resurrection of Jesus, who as our substitute took the penalty for sin (Romans 3:23,24).

**God's path of**

God desires that people turn away from evil.

*Acknowledgment* of sin and *desire to change* are required.

Accept

Reject

**Free Will Choice of**

# . . . He Knew Would Become Evil?

## Why this world is the *best solution* to achieve God's purposes:

1. God wants fellowship with human beings who love Him, so it was necessary for Him to make a world in which people could live, be given the choice to love Him, and be given the opportunity to develop holy character.

2. God wants humans to love Him perfectly. His desire made it necessary that He create a world of totally free choice.

3. The free choice that God granted to human beings also allows them to use His perfect creation for evil. Humans made the choice of evil in the beginning, though they may still turn from evil and choose the good.

4. God has provided a means for imperfect humans to choose to love Him and be forgiven for their past evil. The means He provided for forgiveness were the sacrifice of Himself in the person of His Son, Jesus.

5. Those people who do not accept Jesus' perfect sacrifice and His resurrection (which proves His deity) reject God's love, reject God's forgiveness, and reject Jesus—God—as Lord. Essentially they show disdain, not love, for God.

6. So this world of good and evil is essentially a sorting ground to determine who will choose to seek holiness and love God by freely accepting His gift of forgiveness—by accepting Jesus as *Lord* and *Savior*.

## free-will choices

God desires that all people be saved
(1 Timothy 2:3,4)—
that is, accept forgiveness—
and that they freely love Him as Lord
(Mark 12:30).

↓

Jesus was provided as the perfect sacrifice;
God then raised Him from the dead,
verifying His deity. He can be our
Savior and Lord.

Reject ↓

**Heaven**
Believers can perfectly experience their God-granted holiness and justification (Romans 3:23,24) and are completely free to express perfect love.

Accept →

### Eternal Separation from God

# What Causes Suffering?

We've already established that the existence of human free will allows people to choose evil, which results in suffering for the individual who chooses the evil and usually for other people as well. Are there other causes of suffering?

## Do Satan and Demons Cause Suffering?

It's amazing how many people don't believe in Satan or demons even though the Bible is filled with accounts of their existence. The book of Job gives an excellent picture of how Satan can bring suffering on people. Notice how powerful Satan is:

1. He influenced armies to steal Job's herds and kill his servants (Job 1:14,15).

2. He brought fire from the sky to wipe out Job's sheep and servants (1:16).

3. He influenced raiding parties to steal Job's camels (1:17).

4. He directed a wind that blew down a house, killing Job's children (1:18,19).

5. He inflicted Job with excruciatingly painful sores all over his body (2:7,8).

Satan clearly has enormous power, and he and his demons will create suffering as much as they can. But he still must have God's allowance to exercise his power (Job 1:12; 2:6).

## Does God Ever Cause Suffering?

This idea might initially seem inconceivable—a loving God creating suffering? But before we simply assume that God would never cause suffering, let's consider a few things:

1. **We have a finite mind limited to four dimensions.** Fully understanding the mind of God is impossible for us.

2. **Evil is not the same as suffering.** Evil always has its origin in an intent to do wrong or harm. However, suffering can be caused for

good reasons. For example, people often choose the pain of surgery and recovery in order to have a better functioning body later. And suffering for Christ brings eternal rewards, even though evil may be the cause of the suffering.

3. **God's intentions are much greater than ours.** It's difficult for human beings to look beyond their immediate circumstances. But God always considers the eternal perspective (for example, sometimes our suffering can bring other people to eternal life in Christ).

God is perfectly *holy, loving,* and *just.* To our limited human minds, these attributes often seem to conflict with one another. In fact, from our viewpoint it seems that God sometimes chooses one over the other:

- God struck down Aaron's sons because they used unauthorized fire in the tabernacle (Leviticus 10:1-3). Note that the fire that killed the sons came "from the *presence of the Lord.*" In this case God displayed His *holiness* even though it caused suffering in Aaron's family.
- God struck down David's firstborn son and caused calamity within David's household because of his adultery with Bathsheba and his murder of Uriah, her husband (2 Samuel 12:7-14). Notice again that the Lord said, "*I am going to bring calamity* . . . *I will take your wives and give them to one who is close to you*" (emphasis added). God displayed His justice even though it caused David to suffer.

There are several other cases in the Bible where God caused suffering. But for those people who have accepted Jesus, whatever the source of their difficulty, there is a great message from God:

## The Good News for Christians

"In *all things* God works for the *good of those who love Him, who have been called according to his purpose*" (Romans 8:28, emphasis added). God never wastes a hurt. No matter what the cause of a Christian's suffering, God will use it for some good purpose.

# Are Suffering and Death Always Bad?[9,10,11,12,13]

People often ask why suffering exists. We've all experienced pain at some point in our life, and it usually seems that our suffering has no good purpose. We just want it to be over. Seldom do we actually consider the benefits of pain, suffering, and death.

It is the causes and the justness of pain, suffering, and death that we often understand the least. Sometimes pain and suffering are clearly the result of an evil action (sin)—either our own or another's. For example, a drunk driver causes an auto accident, paralyzing for life both himself and the occupant of the car he crashed into. There seems to be some justice for the one committing the sin of drunkenness, but it's hard to understand why the innocent victim must also suffer.

## The Benefits of Suffering

How can we comprehend the benefits of pain and suffering? Some pain is easy to understand. In fact, it's a protective gift from God. Touch a hot stove, and you learn not to do it again. Feel pain in a part of your body, and you seek a doctor to help you. But long-term suffering is more difficult to understand. Often we don't understand it for many years (see insert on the next page) and sometimes not at all in this life. Some possible benefits of suffering we might not think about when going through it are that God has planned to:

- Teach us something
- Help us learn to love other people
- Test our faith in Him
- Develop our character
- Build our trust in Him
- Inspire us to hope in eternal things

## The Benefits of Death

Most of us think of death as a horrible event—and it is for those people who *refuse to accept Jesus* as Lord and Savior. But for those of us who *do accept* God's love through Jesus, death is a *wonderful* thing! Imagine being transported from a world of evil and unsolvable problems to a perfect paradise where we will live in God's presence forever! What many Christians fear is the suffering that going through the process of death may bring. As awful and drawn-out as it may be, this temporary suffering is still small in comparison to eternity.

# My Own Years of Suffering

Before becoming a Christian, I was a very wealthy man. A few years after becoming a Christian—and shortly before starting my ministry—I lost all my wealth. (Don't assume this will happen to you!) I *now* know God wanted me to focus on Him alone.

The next few years were filled with anxiety, doubts, and depression. I continued to pray and read the Bible daily, which gave me strength. The highlight of my life was my ministry—teaching skeptics the truth of the Bible. I intensely researched the questions and problems of skeptics. (The work of those years has proved invaluable to my teaching today.)

One day, while working on four major "jobs" and facing burn-out, I prayed that God would remove all the jobs that were not part of His plan. Within two weeks, all my income-producing jobs stopped. Only my ministry work remained—which produced *no* income. So I focused solely on the ministry. Then, miracle after miracle occurred, allowing me to keep the ministry going while providing just enough income for my suffering family.

Now, years later, I see some of the purposes of our suffering:

1. I had to learn to *depend on God*, not on my money or my position.

2. I was being *tested in my commitment* to Him.

3. I *learned* to effectively address skeptics' problems and questions.

*Bottom-Line Purpose:* God's purpose for me was ministry. He had to teach me to depend on Him, not on money. He wanted to build my character and teach me to help others. Now, several million people have been impacted by my books, lectures, videos, sermons, seminars, and TV and radio programs. I no longer desire wealth (which is a good thing!). I just want to see others come to know Christ personally.

My suffering had a far-reaching purpose—that of *helping people eternally. Suffering can work for good* (Romans 8:28).

# The Suffering of Jesus

A God who created the universe could certainly have created a world without suffering. But the reasons why He did not—and why the existence of our kind of world makes perfect sense— have already been explored (see pages 18–23). However, some people may think that God is evil and unfeeling because He "sits up there in a perfect paradise" while we are suffering down here. This is far from the truth.

## Don't Forget God's Suffering

God came to earth in the person of Jesus Christ and went through all the types of suffering that most people go through— until about A.D. 32. At that time, Jesus voluntarily exposed himself to the most painful, horrible, and humiliating death ever devised by man: crucifixion.

# What Is Crucifixion?

Invented by the Romans about 400 B.C., crucifixion was designed to be the most horrible death anyone could imagine. It was especially humiliating because victims were hung naked and totally helpless at major road intersections to remind people of the horror they would face if they broke Roman law.

Victims were lashed 39 times with a multi-stranded leather whip that contained chips of glass and sharp pieces of metal. The flesh was torn, often hanging off the backs of victims in large pieces. Sometimes the scourging alone caused death.

In this weakened state, victims were forced to carry a large, very heavy cross to the site of execution. Then large spikes were driven through the wrist area (deemed part of the hand in those days). This area of the body contains a large concentration of nerves, which greatly increases the pain. The feet were likewise nailed into the cross.

Then the cross was hoisted. Whether hanging from the spikes in their wrists or pushing off the spikes in their feet, the victims experienced excruciating pain with every movement. In order to breathe, however, they had to push themselves up with their legs, then lower themselves down again to rest them. Just breathing was an enormously painful process of up and down, up and down; eventually strength would run out and the victims could no longer push themselves up—and they would die of asphyxiation.

Whenever we doubt God's existence—whenever we wonder whether any God worth the name would create a world He knew would be overwhelmed by pain, suffering, and death—we should remember that He chose to enter this world, to suffer more than anyone, and to die in the most painful manner, just to allow us to choose to have eternal life with Him in heaven. Remember:

> God so loved the world that he gave his one and only Son,
> that whoever believes in him shall not perish
> but have eternal life.
> —John 3:16

# The Suffering of Early Christians

Why would a loving God have allowed millions of early Christians to suffer so greatly? After all, His love for those believers who spread the Gospel must have been tremendous. But we know that the early Christians faced the threat of persecution every day.

Written tradition tells us that over a period of about 40 years, 11 of the 12 apostles (all except John) died horrible deaths in order to spread the *historical truth* of the resurrection of Jesus. How do their deaths attest to the resurrection? Consider the fact that the apostles were in a unique position to *know* whether or not the claims about the resurrection were true. Yet rather than renounce the gospel, all but one of them died excruciating deaths for it.

| | |
|---|---|
| Peter—crucified upside down | James—stoned |
| Paul—beheaded | Thaddaeus—shot with arrows |
| Matthew—death by sword | James, son of Zebedee— |
| James, son of Alphaeus— | death by sword |
| crucified | Philip—crucified |
| Simon—crucified | Bartholomew—crucified |
| Thomas—speared | John—natural death |

The horrible suffering that God permitted the apostles to go through gives us tremendous confidence today in the biblical record. If the apostles' trials had been minor, we might question the strength of their belief. But the fact that they knew the truth and knew they would face painful deaths (they all had seen other Christians tortured and killed) attests to their complete certainty about the historical facts of Jesus' life, death, and resurrection. They did not die for a lie.

> The apostles' suffering provided
> the greatest good for the countless people
> who have accepted Christ based on
> the apostles' conviction about the truth.

# Other Early Martyrs

The martyrdom of the early Christians was based on their conviction about *historical fact*. This differs greatly from religions that commend martyrdom for philosophical or mythical ideas that are not rooted in actual events. Christians did not die for supposed or projected beliefs, such as those advocated by the Heaven's Gate cult, Shintoism, or other philosophies.

Many historical sources besides the Bible describe the large numbers of Christian martyrs. These numbers were especially great during the first few hundred years of persecution. Archaeology supports these sources with the discovery of the catacombs under the streets of Rome—some 900 miles of caves containing about 7 million graves, rediscovered in the year 1578. These caves were a hiding and burial place for early Christians who were suffering persecution. Historical accounts give vivid details of these Christians' intense suffering—people were crucified, fed to lions, or impaled on stakes and then set on fire to provide light for Roman orgies.

Most compelling are the many historical references to the "odd attitude" of Christians who were going to such horrid deaths—full of joy and peace. And to avoid the dreadful suffering, "all Christians had to do" was to curse Jesus, renounce Christianity, and bow down to the emperor's statue. It's clear that these Christians, many of whom died as early as the time of the eyewitnesses, truly believed in the gospel.

> Again, their intense suffering provided the greatest
> good for the countless people who accept
> Christ today because of them.

Is it fair that early martyrs (and the many others who have suffered through the centuries) "pay the price" for other people? First of all, remember that God Himself *has already paid the price for all of us* through the death of Jesus Christ. Second, we need to remember that, as humans, we are limited in our thinking to our world of time and three-dimensional space. God can and will reconcile all injustices. In fact, martyrs and sufferers will gain rewards after death, as God tells us. These rewards are so wonderful that we cannot even imagine them (Revelation 21:4,6,7; 22:12).

# Placing Suffering in Perspective

Would it be worth suffering a 30-second vaccine injection to avoid the long-term effects of smallpox? Would you endure a few months of chemotherapy so you could live a long life free of cancer? Sometimes an enormous long-term benefit requires suffering to attain it. Jesus Himself said we would have to suffer to follow Him and obtain eternal life in paradise (Matthew 10:21,22,38,39). Isn't a second or two of suffering worth billions of years—really, an infinity—of an inconceivably wonderful eternity?

## An Eternal Perspective on Suffering

It's obvious God sometimes allows suffering. As indicated earlier (pages 26, 27), God even uses it to accomplish His greater purposes. Whatever suffering we experience during our lives, whether little, much, or every moment of our lives, our human minds are still mostly preoccupied with the present—the here and now. *God is focused on eternity—an eternity of good.*

The point is, what humans regard as unbearable suffering will come to an end and is really a very small part of eternity. *How we deal with that suffering is all-important;* it actually tests us in regard to true love and trust, the love and trust that can be anchored only in God. Consider what the Bible says:

- "Suffering produces perseverance" (Romans 5:3).
- "All this is evidence that God's judgment is right, and as a result you will be counted worthy of the kingdom of God, for which you are suffering" (2 Thessalonians 1:5).
- "This is my gospel, for which I am suffering even to the point of being chained like a criminal. But God's word is not chained" (2 Timothy 2:8,9).
- "In bringing many sons to glory, it was fitting that God, for whom and through whom everything exists, should make the author of their salvation perfect through suffering" (Hebrews 2:10).

- "Remember those earlier days after you had received the light, when you stood your ground in a great contest in the face of suffering" (Hebrews 10:32).
- "Brothers, as an example of patience in the face of suffering, take the prophets who spoke in the name of the Lord. As you know, we consider blessed those who have persevered. You have heard of Job's perseverance and have seen what the Lord finally brought about. The Lord is full of compassion and mercy" (James 5:10,11).

Nothing presented here is intended to minimize the tremendous pain, hurt, and grief that result from suffering. But our lives continue while we are suffering, even though we might wish they would stop; and through it all we need to keep facing the central issues of human existence. We must ultimately realize that God is in control—and that God is loving, God is just, and God is holy. His acts of love, justice, and holiness have been documented over thousands of years. We are not in a position to judge Him. The final answers to suffering lie in a dimension beyond ours—because they lie with God Himself.

Remember—Our entire lifetime, even if it is 100 years of suffering, is like the smallest fraction of a second when compared to billions of years (actually, an infinity) of eternity. Perhaps we should accept God's plan, since He knows both the end and the beginning (Isaiah 46:9,10). He is the One who can help us develop an attitude of joy in suffering, as did the early Christians who came to know Jesus (1 Thessalonians 1:5-10).

# Suffering from Natural Disasters and Accidents

How do we account for suffering that is caused by natural or accidental events, such as earthquakes, volcanoes, or personal mishaps? The Bible does not spell out the ultimate causes of accidents and natural disasters, but in the book of Job, we discover they can be caused by Satan. Notice that God allowed Satan to bring evil upon people (Job 1:12-22).

## Natural Disasters

Only recently has science determined that many natural disasters have a very positive and sometimes necessary role in the operation of the world's ecosystem. For instance, thunderstorms produce lightning, which sometimes accidentally strikes a person (chances: about 6 in 100,000). However, lightning also creates a valuable fertilizer that humans cannot efficiently produce. This fertilizer is important because it helps support the existence of the rain forests that produce much of the oxygen in our atmosphere.

Earthquakes and volcanoes—two other examples that often come to mind—are also important to our environment. Both allow minerals vital for plant growth to come to the earth's surface to replace those that have been depleted. Though the beneficial results of earthquakes are usually localized, volcanic ash can be carried widely through the atmosphere, spreading useful nutrients over enormous distances.

In spite of the benefits they bring, throughout human history natural disasters have mostly been regarded as causes of disruption, suffering, and death—and rightly so. Whether they are caused by Satan for his evil purposes or simply allowed by God as part of His master plan for the world, we can only speculate. Ultimately, we must choose to build our faith and character by trusting in God's complete control, though we may not be able to see or understand His purposes right now.

# Accidental Suffering

It is impossible to fully understand why God allows seemingly random or accidental suffering to happen. Why are some people born with birth defects from which they suffer all their lives? Why do airplanes crash due to undetected mechanical problems? Why would a child accidentally fall into a swimming pool and drown?

We do get some indication of God's intent from Jesus' reply to His disciples when they questioned Him about the blindness of a beggar (John 9:1-5). The disciples believed his blindness had been caused by his own sin, or perhaps even by the sin of his parents. Jesus replied that sin was not the cause (God was not punishing the man for someone's sin, though He had allowed the blindness). Jesus further explained the affliction as a means for the work of God—specifically, the work of Jesus Himself—to be displayed through the man to many other people.

Sometimes we see God's miraculous work in the preservation of people from disasters or accidents: people who survive against all odds or are unexplainably cured of illness. Other times we see the courageous lives of people who have trusted God *through* disaster or accident: those whose bodies are disabled from birth or through accident, parents of children who have lost their lives through mishap or disaster. The works of God are displayed in both of these kinds of people. In the end, we must keep in mind that God unquestionably knows what is best for each of us; not just for us as individuals, but for the other people who are around us.

## Accidents and Disasters Require Us to Acknowledge God's Involvement with Human Beings

1. **Regarding human accidents**—for example, a parent accidentally leaves a door open and a child drowns in a backyard pool. To summarize what we've already looked at, if there is no free-will choice of good or bad, of responsibility or negligence, *then people are nothing*

*more than robots*. If we acknowledge that we have free will, then we must also acknowledge a Designer who created that free will.

2. **Regarding natural accidents**—for example, a tree is blown over and kills a child. First—and this is something we don't often think of—recognize that God could allow many more natural accidents than now occur. He is merciful in everything He does. Second, recognize that Satan's work is behind many things that are evil.

Most importantly, recognize that by allowing *some* accidents, *God make us reckon with His existence.* Jesus made this connection when He spoke of a well-known disaster of His day (a tower had collapsed, killing 18 people—see Luke 13:1-5). He drew two conclusions: first, that the victims had *not* died because they were more sinful than other people (that is, they had not deserved it); and second, that all of his hearers would *also* perish one day unless they turned to God.

For those of us who have turned to God, the unexpected difficulties that come into our lives *encourage the growth of our faith and trust in Him* for the ultimate things. This kind of faith and trust reaches out to God; it reaches beyond the world that we can understand. And in the end, as God has told us, there are some things that we still would never be able to understand, even if He were to explain them to us (Isaiah 55:8,9).

# Why Does God Let Children Suffer?

One of the most heart-wrenching tragedies of life is the suffering of little children and others who in no way seem to deserve it. Imagine the heartache of the parents of a child with incurable leukemia. Or a child paralyzed for life. My wife and I have experienced such pain on a lesser scale; we have a diabetic child who must give himself injections four times a day—possibly for the rest of his life.

Why do we have more compassion for children than for other people who suffer? Perhaps it's because they're young, beautiful, and "innocent"; perhaps it's because they have a full life ahead of them that suffering might blight; perhaps it's due to our God-given protective instinct; perhaps it's some combination of all of these. In any case, the strength of our feeling seems to demand that we find a real explanation for what we see.

But in the face of the suffering of so many children in our world, especially when it's our own children, any reason for it that we can come up with seems insufficient. Indeed, we may simply not be aware—and may never be aware in this life—of the reasons for suffering. Those who believe in the God of the Bible (the authority of which has been demonstrated—see pages 8–11) have the only possible anchor in this situation. They have faith—which is a gift from God—in the ultimate value of both the known and unknown, based on the following:

1. God is all-good.
2. God is all-powerful.
3. Suffering exists.
Therefore:
4. *God has a morally sufficient reason to allow suffering to exist.*[14]

The Scriptures tell us that God has retained "secret" things that only He will know (Deuteronomy 29:29). And as we have seen, in the book of Isaiah God implies that we might not be able to understand some mysteries even if He were to explain them to us (55:8,9). But most important of all, the Bible says many times that God wants us to have faith—faith not in theories or cosmic forces or even in our own ability to reason things out, but faith in Him.

# The Good News

1. God is loving, just, and holy.

2. God loves children and will lovingly and justly address children's suffering (Matthew 18:5,6,10).

3. Life is eternal. A child's suffering today seems very hard—even unbearable—to most people, especially the parents of the afflicted child. But our burden can be lightened by viewing the suffering from the perspective of eternity, knowing that a loving God *will* establish perfect love, justice, and holiness.

## Original Sin—The Origin of Suffering?

Almost all biblical theologians trace suffering back to the original sin of Adam and Eve in the Garden of Eden. In addition to the spiritual death that separated humans from God, physical death also entered the world. God told Eve that, as a result of her and Adam's sin, from then on there would be great pain during childbirth. He told Adam that people's work to provide food for themselves would be painful and toilsome. Then Adam and Eve were banished from the Garden.

Since Adam was the father of the human race, his original sin has caused every child fathered by a man to have a nature that is sinful from the time of conception (Psalm 51:5; Romans 3:23). The Jewish laws for purification of a mother after childbirth may emphasize this—they require a final "atonement for sin" (Leviticus 12:6,7). We know from God's command to "be fruitful and multiply" (Genesis 1:27,28) that He commanded union between a man and a woman; indeed, He pronounced it "very good," along with all else He had made (Genesis 1:31). So if the "sin" did not relate to the physical union, what was the sin offering for? Perhaps it related to the original sin—that everyone is born with a nature that is sinful. Normal observation tells us this. After all, we need to teach our children to be *good*. We never need to teach them to be *bad*.

# Suffering from Grief

At one time or another, nearly everyone grieves from the loss of a loved one or over some sad event. So grief is one of the most common forms of human suffering. Why did God allow the emotion of grief to exist in the first place? Is there any benefit from grief? How does God expect us to react to our grief?

## Grief Is a Demonstration of Love

The Bible frequently depicts grief as a symbol of love. For example, Jesus' disciples were filled with grief when He told them He had to die (Matthew 17:23; John 16:6,7). The Bible also says that, in some cases, grief will be turned to joy, once we realize the eternal benefits of knowing the risen Christ (John 16:20-22). This is very meaningful when a loved one dies who knows Jesus. A husband or wife and family grieve over the loss of that person here on earth...

> ...but they have the ultimate joy of knowing
> they will spend an eternity with that loved one in heaven,
> in God's presence.

## Should We "Pour Out" Our Grief to God?

Grief many times leads to anger, often at God. Is it acceptable to be angry? The Bible says:

> The Lord is close to the brokenhearted and
> saves those who are crushed in spirit.
> —*Psalm 34:18*

The Bible encourages us to pour out our grief to God. Jesus Himself poured out His grief to His Father in the Garden of Gethsemane (Matthew 26:37-39). In Psalm 88, the author speaks to God, vividly portraying his loss, anger, and sadness. When we pray to God, *we should acknowledge our grief*. It draws us closer to Him. He is the One who knows grief the most intimately, because of His Son's death (Mark 15:34; Romans 8:32). And we can be certain He already knows our grief as well.

Psalm 77:7-12 reminds us to rely on the Lord:
"Will the Lord reject forever?
Will he never show his favor again?
Has his unfailing love vanished forever?
Has his promise failed for all time?
Has God forgotten to be merciful?
Has he in anger withheld his compassion?"
Then I thought, "To this I will appeal:"
. . . I will remember the deeds of the Lord;
yes, I will remember your miracles of long ago.
I will meditate on all your works
and consider all your mighty deeds.

## David Grieved *Before* His Son Died

The life of King David gives us great insight into the process and attitude of grieving. The prophet Nathan told David that his son, born of an adulterous relationship with Bathsheba, would die because of David's adultery and his murder of Bathsheba's husband. David grieved greatly— fasting, mourning, lying prostrate on the ground—until the day the child actually died, seven days after he was born (2 Samuel 12:15-19).

David's servants were afraid to tell him his son had died, fearing he would take drastic action. But David surprised them by getting up, washing, eating, and worshiping God (12:20).

When his servants asked him why he had stopped grieving after the child's death, David replied, among other things, "I will go to him, but he will not return to me" (12:23). In spite of his sorrow, *David had faith in God's eternal plan.*

# Attitudes Affect Suffering

It's a well-known fact, supported by the observations of many physicians and by medical studies, that positive attitudes in times of suffering can greatly increase healing from a physical or emotional condition. At the very least, a good attitude can bring positive, beneficial acceptance of a condition or circumstance. We can react to suffering in several ways, ranging from very negative to very positive:

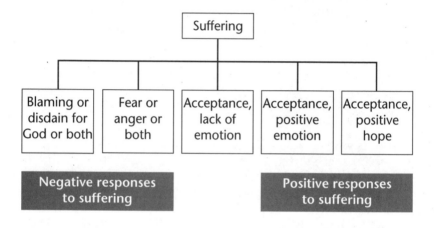

## What the Bible Says...

1. "Now the spirit of the LORD had departed from Saul, and *an evil spirit from the LORD tormented him.* Saul's attendants said to him, 'See, *an evil spirit from God is tormenting you'* " (1 Samuel 16:14,15, emphasis added).

2. "Listen to my prayer, O God, do not ignore my plea; hear me and answer me. *My thoughts trouble me* and I am distraught at the voice of the enemy, at the stares of the wicked; for they bring down suffering upon me and revile me in their anger. My heart is in anguish within me; the terrors of death assail me. *Fear and trembling have beset me*" (Psalm 55:1-5, emphasis added).

3. "In spite of severe suffering, *you welcomed the message with the joy given by the Holy Spirit*" (1 Thessalonians 1:6, emphasis added).

4. "You, however, know all about my teaching, my way of life, my purpose, faith, patience, love, endurance, *sufferings*—what kinds of things happened to me in Antioch, Iconium and Lystra, the persecutions I endured. *Yet the Lord rescued me from all of them*" (2 Timothy 3:10,11, emphasis added).

5. "'Father, if you are willing, take this cup from me; yet not my will, but yours be done.' *An angel from heaven appeared to him and strengthened him*" (Luke 22:42,43).

## Our Choices in Suffering

Regarding our relationship with God, we can essentially choose one of two directions when we go through suffering: We can *draw closer to Him*; or we can *move away from Him*. In the first example on the previous page, Saul drew away from God. He was "tormented." In the second case, David was in deep anguish, yet he still chose to go to God, telling Him exactly how he felt. In the third example, Paul praised the Thessalonians for the joy with which they received the gospel in spite of their suffering. In the fourth case, Paul describes his own suffering and how God rescued him from all these persecutions. In the last example, Jesus is our model of what to do in suffering—turn to God. Though it was God's will to carry forward the plan that required Jesus to suffer, an angel was provided to strengthen Him, helping Him to endure.

# Dealing with Suffering

Here are a few key guidelines for dealing with times of suffering.*

## When You Are Suffering

1. **Talk to God about your suffering**. Be honest. Explain your anguish, your fears, your pain, and your frustration. Ask God to comfort you in your time of trouble. Ask for relief. Don't beg—if you're a Christian, remember that you're God's beloved child, not an outsider. This will help you have faith in God that He will hear your prayer (Luke 11:5-13). Don't bargain. Bargaining implies that you have a degree of equal stature with God. (But what could you ever give the Creator of the entire universe that He needs?) Rather, approach God as His son or daughter, like a little child (Matthew 18:1-5), not in the arrogance of bargaining. God opposes proud people, but He gives grace to those who are humble (1 Peter 5:5-7). Thank God in advance for the help He will provide. Believe that He will do what He has said.

2. **Talk to others about your suffering**. This does not mean telling everyone, then waiting around, hoping for sympathy. Choose a few close friends and share what you're going through. They may have some good advice, or know others who have gone through your pain and can help you. And their listening to you in love and compassion will help you endure.

3. **Focus your thoughts on the things that are true, noble, right, pure, lovely, and admirable**. The Bible tells us not to be anxious about anything, but to pray to and petition God for answers. The Bible then promises peace beyond all understanding for everyone who has accepted Jesus (Philippians 4:6,7).

4. **Recognize that although you may not understand the cause of suffering, God has allowed it for His purpose**.[13] God can use suffering as: 1) a tool for *good* (John 11:49-52); 2) a tool for *change* from evil (Proverbs 20:30); 3) a tool for *teaching* (Hebrews 12:7); 4) a tool to *test* your faith (James 1:6-9); 5) a tool to *improve* you (Genesis 15:13,14); and 6) a tool to *build your character and faith in God* (2 Corinthians 7:9; 1 Peter 4:19).

* Please refer to the Notes and Bibliography for more helpful resources and information.

# When Your Loved Ones or Friends Are Suffering

1. **Listen to their accounts of suffering.** It doesn't matter whether you feel their suffering is trivial or justified, or even that their account is exaggerated. The suffering is real to them. Sometimes what they need most is someone to listen to them (see "Talk to others..." on the previous page).

2. **After much listening, reveal your own times of suffering when appropriate.** If you are a Christian, the greatest strength to get through suffering comes from a strong relationship with Jesus. This offers real hope for anyone. When it's appropriate, tell about the ultimate benefits of suffering in your own life and from the Scriptures. (Personally, I was taught through ten years of difficulty to depend on God, which prepared me for ministry—see page 27).

3. **Be loving; don't discourage grief on the part of the suffering person, and don't hide your own.** A sincerely caring, "nonpreaching" attitude goes a long way in showing love, as does your own sorrow in sympathy with the person you're comforting. Grief is a natural response to suffering. It should be allowed to show rather than be "bottled up" inside. Sometimes people are embarrassed by their grief, and in this case, a loving silence is golden.

4. **If it's clear that someone is dying, look for resources and support.** Your local hospice center will have a wealth of excellent resources and information to help you understand a dying person's physical and emotional needs. Much of this material is based on direct experience and observation, though it's always important to test the material's basic spiritual assumptions against the Word of God.* Local hospitals, as well other organizations, can also be good sources of help.

5. **Do your best to help the suffering person to focus on the positive and on hope—especially hope in Jesus Christ.** Though it's difficult—often extremely difficult—to win through to a positive attitude, it is of enormous benefit to those who are suffering (see "Recognize..." on the previous page; also pages 42, 43).

---

* See *What Really Happens When You Die?* in the *Examine the Evidence* series.

# The Critical Questions

The key conclusions in this book are based on belief in God and the Bible. There is substantial evidence for both (see pages 8–15). Is there any significant evidence to the contrary?

This question is precisely the basis for the entire *Examine the Evidence* series.* Here are some suggestions of additional resources from the series that deal with evidence for the Bible and the existence of God:

**Belief in God:** see *Does the Bible Predict the Future?*—proof for the existence of a supernatural God; *Science—Was the Bible Ahead of Its Time?*—scientific facts contained in the Bible 2000 years before science discovered them; *Creation vs. Evolution*—literal proof that evolution is impossible and a supernatural God created the very concept of design.

**Belief in the Bible:** see *Is the Bible Really a Message from God?*—many reasons why the Bible is uniquely from God; *Can You Trust the Bible?*—thorough evidence that the Bible we have today is virtually the same as the original; *Can Archaeology Prove the New Testament?* and *Can Archaeology Prove the Old Testament?*—much supportive evidence for the Bible.

## How Can We Ensure the Right Relationship So We Can Go to Heaven?

When Jesus said not all who use His name will enter heaven (Matthew 7:21-23), He was referring to people who think using Christ's name along with rules and rituals is the key to heaven. A *relationship* with God is not based on rituals and rules. It's based on grace, forgiveness, and on having the right standing with Him through Jesus Christ.

## How to Have a Personal Relationship with God

1. **B**elieve that God exists and that He came to earth in the human form of Jesus Christ (John 3:16; Romans 10:9).

2. **A**ccept God's free forgiveness of sins through the death and resurrection of Jesus Christ (Ephesians 2:8-10;1:7,8).

3. **S**witch to God's plan for your life (1 Peter 1:21-23; Ephesians 2:1-5).

4. **E**xpress desire for Christ to be director of your life (Matthew 7:21-27; 1 John 4:15).

* The *Examine the Evidence* series is published by Harvest House Publishers and is available through Christian bookstores.

## Prayer for Eternal Life with God

"Dear God, I believe You sent Your Son, Jesus, to die for my sins so I can be forgiven. I'm sorry for my sins, and I want to live the rest of my life the way You want me to. Please put Your Spirit in my life to direct me. Amen."

## Then What?

People who sincerely take these steps become members of God's family of believers. A new world of freedom and strength is available through prayer and obedience to God's will. It is very important to strengthen this new relationship by taking the following initial steps of obedience to God's Word:

- Find a Bible-based church that you like and attend regularly.
- Try to set aside some time each day to pray and read the Bible.
- Locate other Christians to spend time with on a regular basis.

## God's Promises to Believers

### For Today

But seek first His kingdom and His righteousness,
and all these things [things to satisfy all your needs]
will be given to you as well.
—Matthew 6:33

### For Eternity

Whoever believes in the Son has eternal life,
but whoever rejects the Son will not see life,
for God's wrath remains on him.
—John 3:36

**Once we develop an eternal perspective, even the greatest problems on earth fade in significance.**

# Notes

1. Muncaster, Ralph O., *Creation vs. Evolution*, Eugene, OR: Harvest House Publishers, 2000.
2. Muncaster, Ralph O., *Does the Bible Predict the Future?*, Eugene, OR: Harvest House Publishers, 2000.
3. Muncaster, Ralph O., *Science—Was the Bible Ahead of Its Time?*, Eugene, OR: Harvest House Publishers, 2000.
4. Muncaster, Ralph O., *Can You Trust the Bible?*, Eugene, OR: Harvest House Publishers, 2000.
5. Muncaster, Ralph O., *Can Archaeology Prove the Old Testament?*, Eugene, OR: Harvest House Publishers, 2000.
6. Muncaster, Ralph O., *Can Archaeology Prove the New Testament?*, Eugene, OR: Harvest House Publishers, 2000.
7. Muncaster, Ralph O., *What Is the Proof for the Resurrection?*, Eugene, OR: Harvest House Publishers, 2000.
8. Baker, D.R.E., ed., *The Complete Word Study of the Old Testament*, Chattanooga, TN: AMG Publishers, 1994.
9. Warren, Rick, Saddleback Church, *God's Antidote for Dark Valleys*, audiotape. Phone: (949) 829-0300.
10. Warren, Rick, Saddleback Church, *God's Antidote to Your Hurt*, audiotape. Phone: (949) 829-0300.
11. Warren, Rick, Saddleback Church, *How God Heals Your Hidden Wounds*, audiotape. Phone: (949) 829-0300.
12. Warren, Rick, Saddleback Church, *The Season of Loss*, audiotape. Phone: (949) 829-0300.
13. Warren, Rick, Saddleback Church, *The Truth About Your Pain*, audiotape. Phone: (949) 829-0300.
14. Booth, Robert R., ed., Bahnsen, Dr. Greg L., *Always Ready*, Atlanta, GA: American Vision, 1996.

# Bibliography

Baxter, J. Sidlow, *The Other Side of Death*, Grand Rapids, MI: Kregel, 1987.

Elwell, Walter A., ed., *Evangelical Dictionary of Theology*, Grand Rapids, MI: Baker Book House Co., 1984.

Geisler, Norman, and Brooks, Ron, *When Skeptics Ask*, Grand Rapids, MI: Baker Book House Co, 1996.

Hill, Alexander, *Just Business—Christian Ethics for the Modern Marketplace*, Downers Grove, IL: InterVarsity Press, 1997.

Lewis, C.S., *Mere Christianity*, New York, NY: Simon & Schuster, 1980.

*Life Application Bible*, Wheaton, IL: Tyndale House Publishers, and Grand Rapids, MI: Zondervan Publishing House, 1991.

McDowell, Josh, and Wilson, Bill, *A Ready Defense*, San Bernardino, CA: Here's Life Publishers, Inc., 1990.

Muncaster, Ralph O., *Is the Bible Really a Message from God?*, Eugene, OR: Harvest House Publishers, 2000.

Peterson, Michael; Hasker, William; Reichenback, Bruce; and Basinger, David, *Reason & Religious Belief*, New York, NY: Oxford University Press Inc., 1991.

Plantinga, Alvin C., *God, Freedom, and Evil*, Grand Rapids, MI: Eerdmans Publishing Co., 1974.

Smith, F. LaGard, *The Daily Bible in Chronological Order*, Eugene, OR: Harvest House, 1984.

Sproul, R. C., *Now That's a Good Question!*, Wheaton, IL: Tyndale House Publishers Inc., 1996.

Tada, Joni Eareckson, *When God Weeps*, Grand Rapids, MI: Zondervan Publishing House, 1997.